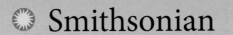
Smithsonian

LITTLE EXPLORER

Airplanes

by Martha E. H. Rustad

CAPSTONE PRESS
a capstone imprint

Little Explorer is published by Capstone Press,
1710 Roe Crest Drive, North Mankato, Minnesota 56003
www.capstonepub.com

For Dad. Fly, baby, fly! —MEHR

Library of Congress Cataloging-in-Publication Data
Rustad, Martha E. H. (Martha Elizabeth Hillman), 1975-
  Airplanes / by Martha E. H. Rustad.
    p. cm. — (Smithsonian little explorer)
  Audience: K-3.
  Summary: "Introduces airplanes to young readers,
including the history and technology
of flight"—Provided by publisher.
  Includes index.
  ISBN 978-1-4765-0248-9 (library binding)
  ISBN 978-1-4765-3542-5 (paper over board)
  ISBN 978-1-4765-3548-7 (paperback)
  ISBN 978-1-4765-3554-8 (ebook PDF)
1. Airplanes—Juvenile literature. I. Title.
  TL547.R87 2014
  629.133'34—dc23   2012050593

Editorial Credits
Kristen Mohn, editor; Sarah Bennett, designer;
Marcie Spence, media researcher; Kathy McColley,
production specialist

Our very special thanks to F. Robert van der Linden,
chairman of the Aeronautics Division at the National Air
and Space Museum, and Paul E. Ceruzzi, chairman of
the Space History Division at the National Air and Space
Museum, for their curatorial review. Capstone would
also like to thank Kealy Wilson, Smithsonian Institution
Project Coordinator and Product Development Manager,
and the following at Smithsonian Enterprises: Ellen
Nanney, Licensing Manager; Brigid Ferraro, Director
of Licensing; Carol LeBlanc, Senior Vice President,
Consumer & Education Products.

Image Credits
Alamy: US Navy Photo, 23 (bottom); Amelia Earhart ®
is a trademark of Amy Kleppner, as heir to the Estate
of Muriel Morrissey, 15; Dreamstime: Brunoil, cover,
Johan63, cover; DVIC, 22 (top); iStockphotos: alxpin, 23
(top), EdStock, 27 (bottom), Hirkophoto, 24; Library of
Congress, 4 (bottom), 10, 11, 12, 14, 16-17; Mary Evans
Picture Library: Grenville Collins Postcard Collection, 17
(bottom); NASA, 27 (top); Shutterstock: Andrew Barker,
4-5, Anthondycz, design element, ART, design element,
B Sanja, design element, B747, 23 (middle), Carlos E.
Santa Maria, 4 (top), Dan Simonsen, 26, Denis Barbulat,
design element, Denise Kappa, 20 (bottom), Everett
Collection, 20 (top), 22 (bottom), EvrenKalinbacak, 8,
Excess, design element, fufam, design element, Ivica
Dobric, design element, Kletr, 13, kstudija, design
element, lkeskinen, design element, Margo Harrison,
6-7, Mikael, Damkier, 21, Mikhail Starodubov, 19 (left),
mountainpix, 18, NEGOVURA, design element, Peteri,
25, (top), Pierre-Yves, Babelon, 8-9, pinyoj, design
element, Seamartini Graphics, design element, spirit
of america, 32, Taqjne, design element, Taras Vyshnya,
1, Tom Klimmeck, 18-19, Vlad Moses, 9, Vlad Siaber,
Boyagerix, 25 (bottom), Willy DFeganello, 5, Yuri Arcurs,
19 (right); Virgin Galactic, 28, 29; Wikipedia, 17 (top)

Printed in the United States of America in Brainerd, Minnesota.
032013   007721BANGF13

TABLE OF CONTENTS

TAKE OFF!

Imagine you are a pilot. Climb in your airplane and put on your seatbelt.

Do your safety check and take off!

In 1903 the first airplane flew for 12 seconds.

You lift above the buildings, trees, and people.

If you were a pilot, where would you fly?

At this minute about 7,000 airplanes are flying over the United States.

5

AIRPLANE PARTS

Some airplanes have a propeller that the engine turns.

Pilots sit in the cockpit and move controls to fly the plane.

The engine gives the plane power.

Wheels move the airplane on the ground.

6

HOW AIRPLANES WORK

Many parts work together to make an airplane fly.

The engine of the plane pulls it forward.

jet engine

The wings help lift the plane off the ground.

The wings and the engine work together to keep the plane in flight.

The thrust of the engine
and the shape of the wings create **LIFT**,
which makes the plane go up.

THRUST is the
force that moves
a plane against
the drag.

DRAG is the air
pushing against
the plane as it
moves forward.

The **WEIGHT** of an
airplane pulls it to Earth.

Aerodynamics is the study of how things fly.

THE WRIGHT FLYER

Brothers Orville and Wilbur Wright owned a bicycle shop. They wanted to build a flying machine.

They studied and built gliders.

The Wright brothers tested as many as 200 wing shapes.

"SUCCESS FOUR FLIGHTS THURSDAY MORNING ... "

—from the telegram the brothers sent to their father after the first flight

Together they built a machine they called a flyer.
In 1903 Orville flew it 200 feet (61 meters).
Then Wilbur flew it 852 feet (260 m).

The Wright brothers had invented the airplane.

The Wright brothers' first flights were in North Carolina. They chose a windy place to help lift the wings. Sand covered the ground for soft landings.

The 1903 *Flyer* is at the National Air and Space Museum in Washington, D.C.

11

BIPLANES

Many early airplanes had two sets of wings. These are called biplanes.

Two wings help lift biplanes into the air.

Early airplanes had open cockpits. Pilots wore warm clothes, helmets, and goggles.

Aerobatics are stunts performed in the air with trick planes.

Some pilots today fly biplanes in air shows.

MAKE A PAPER AIRPLANE

1.
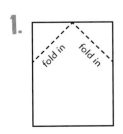
fold in   fold in

2.
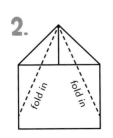
fold in   fold in

3.
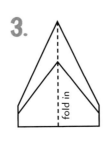
fold in

4.
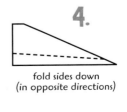
fold sides down
(in opposite directions)

5.
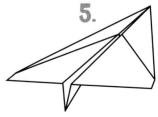

FAMOUS PILOTS

In 1927 Charles Lindbergh flew from New York to Paris. He was the first pilot to fly alone across the Atlantic Ocean.

Lindbergh's flight took more than 33 hours.

Lindbergh let cold air blow on his face to keep him awake during his long flight.

Lindbergh's plane was named *Spirit of St. Louis*. It is at the National Air and Space Museum in Washington, D.C.

Amelia Earhart was a famous American aviator.

In 1932 she flew from Newfoundland to Ireland.

Her flight lasted almost 15 hours.

In 1937 Earhart disappeared while trying to fly around the world.

PASSENGER PLANES

The first airplanes had room for only the pilot.

Later airplanes had room for passengers and cargo.

Passengers get off an airliner in the 1930s.

In 1914 an airline company called St. Petersburg-Tampa Airboat Line flew between the two Florida cities. Carrying one passenger at a time, planes flew twice a day. The flight cost $5 each way.

The earliest airliners were not heated. Passengers had to wear warm clothes.

In 1908 Charles Furnas was the first airplane passenger. He was the Wright brothers' mechanic.

Passengers fly in airplanes
of all sizes today.

Small private planes hold
only a few passengers.

The Airbus A380
is the largest airliner.

It holds up to 800 passengers.

A private plane is owned by a person or a business.
Private planes may be large or small.

The Airbus A380
is almost as long
as a football field.

CARGO PLANES

In 1918 planes carried the first U.S. airmail.

They flew from New York to Philadelphia to Washington, D.C.

Today airplanes carry mail and other packages around the world.

On large cargo planes, the nose opens.

Workers slide big boxes inside.

Cargo planes can carry small boxes, huge semitrailers, and even other aircraft!

MILITARY PLANES

The military began using airplanes soon after they were invented.

Planes allowed the military to travel quickly.

Pilots dropped bombs, shot bullets, or spied on enemies.

bombers

fighter

A fighter plane attacks a group of enemy bombers.

The military flies drone aircraft by remote control. Pilots stay safely on land while controlling drones in the sky.

Today military pilots fly stealth aircraft.

Radar cannot find them.

Some military planes take off from and land on huge ships called aircraft carriers.

23

JETS

By the 1940s some
aircraft were powered
by a new engine called a jet.

Jet engines pull air in through the front.
They push gases out the back.
This action moves an airplane forward.

Jet planes don't need propellers.

Jets fly faster than propeller planes.

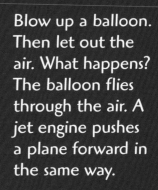

Blow up a balloon. Then let out the air. What happens? The balloon flies through the air. A jet engine pushes a plane forward in the same way.

SUPERSONIC PLANES

The speed of sound is 760 miles (1,223 kilometers) per hour. This speed is called Mach 1.

Supersonic planes fly faster than the speed of sound. This creates a loud booming sound.

Many military planes are supersonic.

In 2004 the NASA X–43A plane flew at Mach 9.6. That is 7,000 miles (11,300 km) per hour!

The Concorde was a famous supersonic passenger airplane. It flew twice the speed of sound.

SPACE PLANES

A space plane can fly above Earth's atmosphere.

Space planes fly at hypersonic speeds. Hypersonic is five times the speed of sound.

SpaceShipTwo is a passenger space plane. People who aren't astronauts can fly to space in it.

A large airplane carries SpaceShipTwo high into the air. It is called a mother ship. Rockets then launch SpaceShipTwo into space.

mother ship

SpaceShipTwo

DO YOU DREAM OF FLYING A SPACE PLANE SOMEDAY?

GLOSSARY

airliner—a large airplane that carries passengers

atmosphere—the mixture of gases that surrounds Earth

aviator—pilot; a person who flies an aircraft

cargo—goods carried on a ship, aircraft, train, or truck

cockpit—the place where a pilot sits in a plane

drone—an unmanned military aircraft that is controlled from the ground

glider—a lightweight aircraft that flies by floating and rising on air currents instead of by engine power

hypersonic—a speed greater than five times the speed of sound

mechanic—someone who fixes vehicles or machinery

nose—the front of an airplane

passenger—a person who rides on an airplane, train, or other vehicle

pilot—a person who flies an aircraft

propeller—a rotating blade that moves a vehicle through water or air

radar—a device that uses radio waves to track the location of objects

semitrailer—a trailer that attaches to a truck tractor for moving goods on the ground

stealth—having the ability to move without being seen by radar

CRITICAL THINKING USING THE COMMON CORE

Describe the features found on most airplanes. What purpose does each feature serve? (Key Ideas and Details)

Look at the diagram on page 9. How does the diagram help explain the text? (Craft and Structure)

What can you learn about SpaceShipTwo's mother ship from the photo on page 28? (Integration of Knowledge and Ideas)

READ MORE

Hamilton, Robert M. *On a Plane.* Going Places. New York: Gareth Stevens, 2012.

Ruck, Colleen. *Planes.* My Favorite Machines. Mankato, Minn.: Smart Apple Media, 2012.

Schaefer, Lola M. *Airplanes in Action.* Transportation Zone. Mankato, Minn.: Capstone Press, 2012.

INTERNET SITES

FactHound offers a safe, fun way to find Internet sites related to this book. All of the sites on FactHound have been researched by our staff.

Here's all you do:

Visit *www.facthound.com*

Type in this code: 9781476502489

Check out projects, games and lots more at
www.capstonekids.com

INDEX